Feng Shui Fundamentals

Education

I dedicate this book with
love, respect, and devotion
to **Lama Zopa Rinpoche**
my dearest kind lama.

To **Jennifer Too** my
darling daughter,
and in accordance with
Rinpoche's request, to the
ultimate happiness of all
sentient beings of the world.

Feng Shui Fundamentals

Education

Lillian Too

ELEMENT

Shaftesbury, Dorset • Rockport, Massachusetts • Melbourne, Victoria

First published in Great Britain by
ELEMENT BOOKS LIMITED
Shaftesbury, Dorset SP7 8BP

Published in the USA in 1997 by
ELEMENT BOOKS INC.
PO Box 830, Rockport, MA 01966

Published in Australia in 1997 by
ELEMENT BOOKS LIMITED
and distributed by Penguin Australia Ltd
487 Maroondah Highway, Ringwood, Victoria 3134

Designed and created with
THE BRIDGEWATER BOOK COMPANY LIMITED

ELEMENT BOOKS LIMITED
Editorial Director Julia McCutchen
Managing Editor Caro Ness
Production Director Roger Lane
Production Sarah Golden

THE BRIDGEWATER BOOK COMPANY LIMITED
Art Director Terry Jeavons
Designer James Lawrence
Managing Editor Anne Townley
Project Editor Andrew Kirk
Editor Linda Doeser
Picture Research Julia Hanson
Studio Photography Guy Ryecart
Illustrations Isabel Rayner, Andrew Kulman, Mark Jamieson,
Michaela Blunden, Paul Collicutt, Olivia Rayner, Jackie Harland

Printed and bound in Hong Kong

British Library Cataloguing in Publication Data available

Library of Congress Cataloging in Publication data available

ISBN 1 86204 120 2

The publishers wish to thank the following for the use of pictures:
Bridgeman Art Library, pp 43; Elizabeth Whiting Associates, pp 11, 32; Julia Hanson, pp 22;
Rex, pp 42; and Zefa, pp 7, 12, 13, 16, 34, 40, 46.

Special thanks go to:
Bright Ideas, Lewes, East Sussex
for help with properties

Lillian Too's website addresses are
http://www.asiaconnect.com.my/lillian-too
http://www.dragonmagic.com

Lillian Too's email addresses are
ltoo@dragonmagic.com
ltoo@popmail.asiaconnect.com.my

CONTENTS

INTRODUCTION TO FENG SHUI

WHAT IS FENG SHUI ?

風水

This ancient Chinese practice is the science of spatial arrangement to create the most harmonious and auspicious surroundings in our living and work places. Feng shui teaches us how to orient homes, offices, doorways, and windows to achieve this balance, and it gives interior decoration guidelines on the display of objects, the best arrangement of furniture, the use of lighting, and the careful selection of color.

At the practical level, feng shui talks about the effect of plants, design motifs, and other symbols – all within the context of its underlying principles. These encompass the Chinese view of the universe, which relies on the balance of yin and yang forces, as well as the productive and destructive cycles of the five elements. Feng shui technology is based on the interpretation of ancient symbols that comprise the eight-sided Pa Kua, with its eight trigrams, and the nine-sector Lo Shu grid of numbers.

THE COSMIC BREATH

Central to these interpretations is the concept of intangible life forces that exist in the atmosphere, what feng shui refers to as the dragon's cosmic breath or sheng chi. This auspicious breath is said to bring various manifestations of great good fortune and the aim of feng shui is to ensure that our living and work spaces are drenched with sheng chi. This is achieved by carefully orienting homes to balance harmoniously with the contours and terrain of surrounding structures in the environment. Blending buildings harmoniously with natural and artificial structures in the landscape, following feng shui guidelines, and taking proper note of heights, hills, other buildings, roads, and waterways promises good fortune, health, and happiness.

A simple houseplant, if positioned according to feng shui guidelines, can attract good fortune into your living space.

Getting your feng shui right brings enormous luck, but getting things wrong literally invites misfortune. Often people are not even aware of this. Some knowledge of this wonderful science can therefore be tremendously useful. Feng shui also shows us how to avoid, deflect, and dissolve the killing breath or shar chi, that exists in the environment alongside the auspicious breath. A basic knowledge of feng shui alerts the practitioner to offensive structures that cause this killing breath, and suggests ways to defuse its pernicious effects. Viewed from this perspective, feng shui is simple to understand and when you have the basic principles it is easy to put them into practice. Feng shui does not need to be difficult, complex, or profound, although it can be, if you wish to delve deeper.

The promise of feng shui is exciting because it can be practiced at many different levels. It addresses every aspect of humankind's multiple aspirations. Feng shui can attract good fortune in the form of enormous success luck – wealth, power, position, fame, love, and more. Good feng shui also holds out the promise of a contented happy family life, just as it can also bring excellent luck to those seeking knowledge. Feng shui supplements the luck of our destinies and boosts the luck we create for ourselves. Feng shui does not work in a vacuum because it is not magic. It supplements human effort with a dose of intangible good fortune luck that leads to achievement and success.

This book deals with specific feng shui guidelines, which produce good fortune in examination luck, bringing with it the attainment of knowledge. There are tips for orienting personalized directions that assist in the process of study. The beneficial energies also create self-motivation and an attitude to success that leads to attainment and achievement. This aspect of feng shui is especially apt for ambitious students.

Feng shui can strengthen the effectiveness of good study habits and ensure educational success.

THE CHINESE VIEW OF EDUCATION

Chinese history is filled with stories about scholars. In ancient China, the path to high office and probably the only way for young men from humble backgrounds to positions of power was to pass the Imperial exams. Attaining a high level of scholarship was metaphorically likened to the lowly carp successfully crossing the Dragon Gate and transforming into a dazzling dragon.

The legend of the dragon carp accurately encapsulates the Chinese attitude toward education, which is one of deep respect. Right up to today, the most important thing to Chinese families throughout the world is that their children should excel in their studies. Like their ancestors of old, they see the scholastic route as the most efficient way of improving their status and their lifestyle. It is hardly surprising that immigrant Chinese in the United States, Britain, and all over Southeast Asia place the attainment of tertiary qualifications by their children as the number one priority in their young lives. A high-quality education has always been considered the universal key to success.

Getting a tertiary education is regarded as the necessary first step in their path to prosperity. Success in exams is viewed as more than a mere end in itself. It is the vital first step in carving out a substantial life and career.

THE ROLE OF FENG SHUI.

It is hardly surprising that one of the most important dimensions of feng shui practice focuses not just on the next generation (the descendants), but more specifically on their attainment of knowledge, which manifests itself in conspicious success at examinations. In the modern context this can be interpreted as getting

good grades all the way through school and into university.

Indeed, there are specific feng shui recommendations that directly address this matter of crossing the Dragon Gate. Both form school and compass feng shui offer exciting methods and guidelines, which are easy to implement, to benefit your children's scholastic career.

THE NATURE OF STUDY LUCK

Today's educational process is as demanding as that of the old days of Imperial China and given the huge competition for university places, excellent examination grades have become immensely important. In the face of all the things that can go wrong, a little help from good feng shui cannot be anything other than welcome. Activating study luck can help remove some of the examinaton hurdles that every student faces, but it is not magic. Remember that it does not automatically turn your child into a straight A student, but with good feng shui, efforts pay off and hard work will show real results. Feng shui is the luck from the earth. If your child complements it with the luck created by his or her own efforts, quantum leaps in achievement will definitely be experienced.

The humble carp, successfully crossing the Dragon Gate and transforming into the magnificent dragon, symbolizes the humble scholar passing the Imperial exams, thereby setting forth on the path to power and high position.

THE PRINCIPLES OF FENG SHUI

The effective use of feng shui requires a basic understanding of the simple, fundamental principles that form the theoretical underpinnings of this fascinating science. This book addresses the concepts that enable a beginner to get the basics right. Simple feng shui can be done on your own once you understand these concepts and it really is not necessary to seek out a feng shui consultant to get your study luck feng shui correct.

YIN AND YANG IN FENG SHUI

The cosmology of yin and yang in Chinese thought maintains that everything in the universe is representative of one of these two opposing but complementary forces. In feng shui these two forces must be in optimum balance for the energies in the surroundings to be at their most auspicious.

Yin is represented by darkness, night time, cold, winter, quiet, stillness, and death. The forces of yin are negative and reminiscent of the moon and the female.

Yang is just the opposite. It is represented by brightness, sunlight, warmth, activity, energy, sounds, and the heat of summer. It also signifies life and the living, as well as maleness. The sun is the ultimate yang symbol.

Yin feng shui refers to the houses of the dead – the cemetery and locations of ancestral graveyards. Although this is a very powerful branch of feng shui, this book does not discuss it further but deals instead with yang feng shui.

YANG FENG SHUI

Yang feng shui refers to the dwellings of the living and it is this kind of feng shui that is referred to when we talk about it generally. In yang feng shui the forces of yang become important, so that rooms alive with healthy yang energy are said to benefit from the vital life force so essential to good feng shui. However, the nature of yin and yang cosmology is such that an excess of yang would create an imbalance, causing bad feng shui.

This is because of the nature of the relationship between yin and yang; the existence of one depends on the other. Without yin, there cannot be yang. Thus without cold, there is no such thing as warmth, without winter, there can be no concept of summer, and without night, how can there be day?

A bedroom should not be painted completely red with red rugs and red bed sheets. This would be interpreted as an excess of yang energy. Similarly, if there are bright spotlights constantly kept on, the energy would be too yang for the bedroom. If the bedroom has a window directly exposed to the western sun, then the glare is too strong. The excess of yang makes the occupant of the room very energetic. The mind becomes far too active and sleep suffers. Such a scenario is not conducive to good study luck.

Thus to enjoy good feng shui, rooms and houses should have a mix or balance of both yin and yang. An excess of yin suggests stillness, stagnation, and even death, while an excess of yang suggests hyperactivity. However, while it is important to guard against excesses of both forces, you should be extra careful with a surfeit of yin energy. Rooms that are too dark and too quiet are lifeless and do not have sufficient life energy.

PRACTICAL ASPECTS OF YIN AND YANG DIAGNOSIS

Growing children need yang energy, but they also need yin energy when they sleep. Thus their rooms should essentially be bright, airy, and filled with life. This can be achieved using sounds (a music system), a bright color scheme (drapes, rugs, quilts) or paintings and pictures that show life, but of course this should not be done to excess.

THE THEORY OF THE FIVE ELEMENTS

Every reference to the Chinese metaphysical and divinatory sciences, including acupuncture, martial arts, fortune telling, medicine, and feng shui, applies both the theory of yin and yang balance and the theory of the five elements. Indeed, every classical text on feng shui contends that all things in the universe, tangible or intangible, can be categorized as one of the five elements. These elements are said to reflect the seasons of the earth as well as the directions of the compass.

The elements are fire, wood, water, metal, and earth and they are said to interact with each other in never-ending productive or destructive cycles. This is said to mirror the interactive nature of all things within the universe. Element analysis must always be applied to feng shui practice. This requires a thorough understanding of how the element cycles work and how they may be applied in a practical way.

SIGNIFICANCE OF THE ELEMENT CYCLES

The diagrams illustrate the two major cycles of the elements, but from these two cycles it is possible to extract various attributes of each of the elements. Thus, if we take the element earth as an example, we can see its attributes.

PRODUCTIVE CYCLE

This illustration shows the productive cycle of the five elements - earth, metal, water, wood, and fire. Fire, the element that produces earth, is in a positive position in relation to earth and is therefore helping to energize earth, which is associated with education and study success.

DESTRUCTIVE CYCLE

This illustration shows the destructive cycle of the five elements. Earth is being overwhelmed by wood, the element that destroys earth. This means that earth, which is associated with education and study luck, is not being strengthened.

- Earth is produced by fire, so fire is said to be good for earth.
- Earth produces metal, so earth is said to be exhausted by metal.
- Earth is destroyed by wood, so wood is said to be bad for earth.
- Earth destroys water, so earth is said to overcome water.

The practice of feng shui involves working with the elements and if earth is the element with which we need to work, understanding its basic attributes, as indicated by the cycles of relationships, makes the practice a lot easier. Elements become significant when we use any of the compass formula methods of feng shui. The element that is associated with each of the eight compass directions of the Pa Kua (see pages 14–15) is determined by the trigram placed on each of its sides. In the compass, the elements fire and water appear only once, while the other three elements – wood, earth, and metal – appear twice in big and small forms.

- Fire is representative of the south.
- Water is representative of the north.
- Big wood belongs to the east, while small wood belongs to the southeast.
- Big metal belongs to the northwest, while small metal belongs to the west.
- Big earth belongs to the south-west, while small earth belongs to the northeast.

THE PA KUA

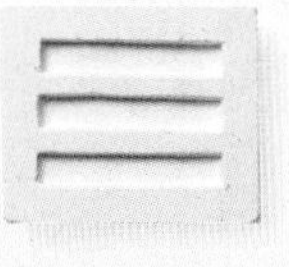

Chien *Northwest*

Kun *Southwest*

Ken *Northeast*

Li *South*

Feng shui derives many of its practical guidelines from the eight-sided Pa Kua symbol. Each side of the Pa Kua occupies 45 degrees of the compass and represents one of the eight compass directions. In accordance with Chinese tradition, the direction south is placed at the top. This placement is very significant since the meanings and attributes of all the directions are determined from the eight trigrams that are placed round the Pa Kua.

These trigrams were derived from the Chinese classic called the I Ching, or the Book of Changes, and they are three

THE LO SHU SQUARE

Another important symbol of feng shui is the Lo Shu square. This is a nine-sector grid, each square of which contains a number from one to nine. The numbers are arranged in the grid in such a way that any three adjoining numbers make the sum of 15, which is also the number of days it takes the moon to grow from new to full. The Chinese believe this is a magic square and that it provides the key to unlocking many of the secrets of the Pa Kua.

Chen *East* **Kan** *North* **Sun** *Southeast* **Tui** *West*

symbolic lines. These lines are either solid unbroken yang lines or broken yin lines. There are eight combinations of broken and unbroken lines.

The corresponding elements of the sides of the Pa Kua are derived from these trigrams, based on the theory of five elements (see pages 12–13).

Practical feng shui thus involves studying directions, trigrams, and elements. It is only when you understand how these basic symbols of feng shui relate to each other that you can correctly put them into practice.

It is believed that the **Lo Shu square** appeared thousands of years ago on the back of a turtle, which emerged from the river Lo. This square features prominently in feng shui technology, particularly in some of the more advanced formulas. Practical feng shui uses this square to demarcate the layout of a room for the easy application of feng shui guidelines and formulas.

There are two arrangements of the trigrams around the Pa Kua: the Early Heaven Arrangement and the Later Heaven Arrangement. The Pa Kua shown here is the Pa Kua of the Later Heaven Arrangement, which is always the arrangement that is used in yang feng shui.

THE MAJOR SYMBOLS OF EDUCATION SUCCESS

KEN

The trigram that symbolizes knowledge and education is Ken, which essentially stands for late winter or early spring. It suggests a time of preparation upon which future success depends. Ken also suggests contemplation, meditation, and the development of the mind. When the energies within the home or room are harmonious within the corners that represent this trigram, excellent education luck can be activated.

THE DIRECTION NORTHEAST

教育

Based on the Later Heaven Arrangement of trigrams around the Pa Kua, the compass direction that represents the trigram Ken is the northeast. Thus to activate education and study luck, it is necessary to energize the northeast. The first thing to see is if there is a true northeast corner of the house. When houses are L- or U-shaped, certain corners appear to be missing and if this happens to be the northeast sector of the house, then feng shui suggests that the education luck of the home is generally lacking. While this can be unfortunate, there is no real cause for alarm.

Mark out the northeast corner using a compass. In this example, the northeast is marked out in yellow based on the compass reading shown. This will be the corner of the bedroom to activate.

Go to the bedroom of the person whose education luck needs activating. This will usually be the bedroom of a child or young person who is still a student. Other rooms used by the entire family can also be activated. The first thing to do, if you wish your child to benefit from study luck, is to stand in the center of his or her bedroom and identify the northeast corner. Use the Lo Shu square as a guide for doing this. Divide the room into nine equal spaces. The bedroom does not need to be square. Two examples of doing this are shown here.

This is an irregular-shaped room, where the southwest is missing, and the south is partly missing. If the northeast corner had been missing, it would have meant an absence of education luck for the occupant of the room. The corner to be activated – the northeast – is drawn out in yellow. Note the method of demarcating the room into nine sectors.

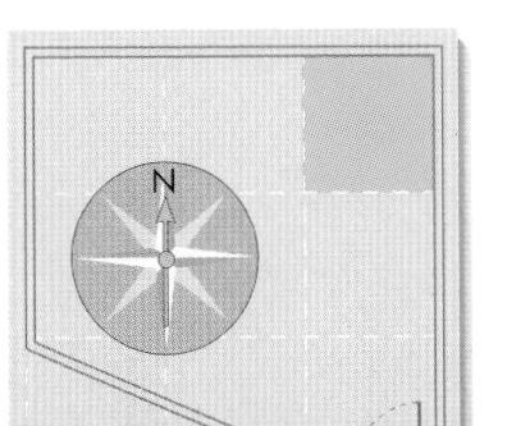

THE ELEMENT EARTH

The element of the northeast is earth. This is derived from the trigram Ken, which means mountain. Thus the element referred to is small earth, and to activate this corner, anything that symbolizes earth can be used. At the same time, we have seen from the cycles of the elements (see page 12–13) that fire produces earth. This means that anything that symbolizes fire can also be used to energize the northeast. Earth produces metal and this means that metal exhausts earth. Metal would, therefore, not be a good energizer for this corner. It is inadvisable to place anything made of metal, including windchimes and bells, in the northeast corner. Finally, anything that belongs to the wood element should not be placed here, since wood destroys earth. This means that plants and flowers in the northeast will spoil your study luck.

ENERGIZING THE NORTHEAST WITH EARTH ELEMENT OBJECTS

The best way of energizing excellent study luck for the students in your family is to focus on energizing the north-east corner of their rooms with feng shui element therapy. Since the element of this corner is earth, displaying earth objects would effectively raise the chi to benefit their studies.

Place the work desk in the northeast of the room and place a crystal on it. This can be either a natural quartz crystal or a handmade lead crystal paperweight. Natural crystals are believed to have great retentive powers. Studying with the crystal nearby taps into the feng shui luck of the earth and the crystal itself will aid efficient study. In a later section of this book (see pages 36–7), you can find out how to check the personal self-development direction of your children, and when you have this information, you should arrange the desk so that your child sits facing his or her best study direction.

CRYSTALS

Place the desk in the northeast corner of the room and place a crystal on the northeast corner of the desk.

A natural quartz crystal is an ideal companion for every student who wishes to activate the earth element for good feng shui. These crystals come from deep within the earth's crust and are excellent purveyors of earth luck. Available from many museum or specialist shops, they are usually quite inexpensive.

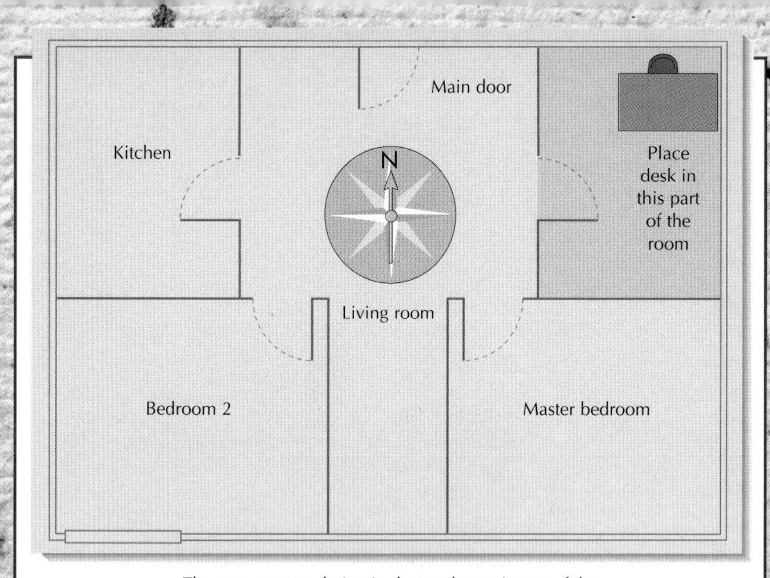

The corner room, being in the northeast, is one of the more suitable rooms for students since this corner symbolizes education and knowledge luck.

USING OTHER OBJECTS

Placing a decorative urn made of clay or any kind of pottery in the northeast is also excellent. It can be the northeast of the garden, the whole house, or the bedroom. Keep the urn empty so that good luck chi may accumulate and settle. Remember that this is the corner of small earth, so it is not necessary to place too large an urn.

Cut glass or crystal balls are also excellent activators when they are hung in the northeast, especially if there is a window and the facets catch the morning sunlight. This creates wonderful yang energy for the room and is especially auspicious.

LIGHTS AND LAMPS

A study lamp is excellent feng shui, but it is advisable to select it carefully. Try to avoid lamps that come in high-tech shapes that look threatening, for example, those with pointed ends or which are shaped in a hostile way. It is far better to choose a lamp that is rounded rather than angular. Do not use spotlights, as the yang energy then becomes too strong. A simple free-standing or hanging lamp is all that you require.

CRYSTAL CHANDELIERS

If you can afford it, perhaps the best way of energizing the northeast or any other earth corner of the home (the southwest and the center of the home) is to hang a beautiful crystal chandelier, as this combines the elements of earth and fire. Chandeliers with crystal pendants also attract sheng chi into the home when hung in the hall just in front of the main entrance door. If you cannot afford a crystal chandelier, shop for a cheaper substitute. Glass is as effective as crystal, as it is also of the earth element.

As an earth supplement, red furnishings and decorations are very effective, as the colour red symbolizes the fire element.

THE COLOR RED

This is an excellent way of supplementing earth with fire. Use red in drapes, cushions, or rugs, but never overdo it by painting entire walls in red since this will overwhelm the room. In feng shui less is better, as balance is essential. If the fire symbol is overdone, it will turn dangerous and burn you. In fact, this is true of every one of the five elements.

DESIGN MOTIFS

There are so many designs and motifs that can symbolize the fire element that you can be as creative as you wish. Designs that feature the sun or are created in red and yellow would be suitable. Again let balance prevail and if in doubt, have less rather than more.

STRENGTHENING THE EARTH ELEMENT WITH FIRE OBJECTS

Since fire produces earth in the cycle of element relationships, any kind of symbolic fire will strengthen the earth element, creating exactly the kind of auspicious flow of energy required. The element of fire is symbolized by all kinds of lights, sun motifs, and the color red. These are the common symbols that are also extremely easy to incorporate into the decor of any room.

ENERGIZING WITH OTHER SYMBOLS OF EDUCATION SUCCESS

Much of feng shui is very symbolic, which is why the Chinese have so many different emblems and gods that personify various aspects of human aspirations. There are gods of wealth and longevity, and symbols of fertility and purity, of undying love, and the attainment of affluence and power. And as you would expect, feng shui also has symbols of supreme educational success.

Practitioners of feng shui can choose to use the Chinese symbols or they may use, equally successfully, symbols that strongly suggest educational success to them. Hence hanging pictures and crests of universities along the education wall (the northeast wall) can be very effective. So, too, is displaying any diplomas, qualifications or awards which reveal your parents' achievements. This attracts knowledge chi into a household that demonstrates what a profound respect it has for education. In this way, the parents' success will be guaranteed to continue to the next generation.

THE WHITE ELEPHANT

This is one of the great treasures of Buddhism and in Thailand the elephant is regarded as a sacred animal. It is a symbol of strength, prudence, and sagacity. Displayed in the home, the feng shui significance borders on the almost superstitious belief that it aids the sons of a family in gaining recognition through determination and prudence. This belief is widespread in Vietnam and Cambodia, where ceramic white elephants are a popular feature of most homes. Place them in pairs just outside the doorway.

The white elephant personifies the virtues of strength, prudence. and sagacity. This powerful symbol is found in many homes in the East.

THE DRAGON CARP

The Chinese regard this as the most potent symbol of education and career success. The symbol is that of a creature with the tail of a carp and the head of a dragon, which symbolizes the humble carp transforming into a dragon. Dragon carps, which can be ceramic or made of wood, are usually displayed in pairs placed on either side above the entrance into the home. This symbolizes that each time the residents go out of the home to face the world they become brave and clever dragons! The dragon carp crossing the Dragon Gate is thus also very popular for activating career luck.

THE FOUR PRECIOUS TREASURES

Also referred to as the invaluable gems of the literary apartment, the four treasures are ink, paper, brush pen, and ink slab. When present in the home, these items signified the presence of a learned man. Thus, in the old mansions of Chinese mandarins, they were always specially displayed with great care, and in most instances, were of the finest quality. Chinese ink was usually stored in solid form, hence the ink slab. Paper was often made from the finest rice straw, while the brush pen was made of sable, fox, or rabbit hairs set in a bamboo holder. If you display these four items in your home, it is believed that at least one of your children will gain the highest scholastic achievements.

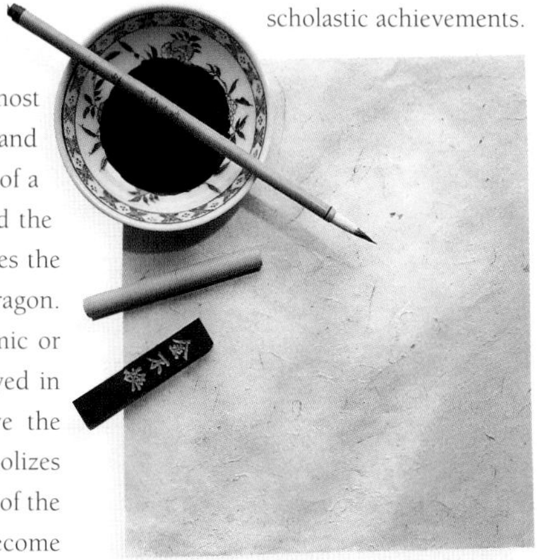

Ink, paper, brush pen, and ink slab are displayed in the home to assure educational success.

PERSONALIZED STUDY ORIENTATIONS

THE COMPASS FORMULA

學習

Each person has an individual, self-development direction called the Fu Wei direction. You can calculate the Fu Wei of your children using an old and powerful compass school formula. It uses the date of birth and the technique was, for many years, a closely guarded secret. Known as the Pa Kua Lo Shu formula (or Kua formula), it was given to the author's feng shui master by an old Taiwan grand master who was a legend in his time. The formula was derived from the two principal symbols of feng shui – the eight-sided Pa Kua, with its many levels of meanings, and the Lo Shu, the nine-sector grid, which is also known as the magic square.

According to feng shui, each person has four lucky and four unlucky directions, depending on whether he or she is an east or west group person. Which group you belong to is determined by your year of birth and gender. Once you know the personal auspicious Fu Wei direction of your child, you can make use of the information in many different ways that will greatly enhance his or her personal feng shui luck.

It can be used with equal success in the various rooms of the home, the classroom, in school, and at college. Using the direction implies sleeping and sitting in

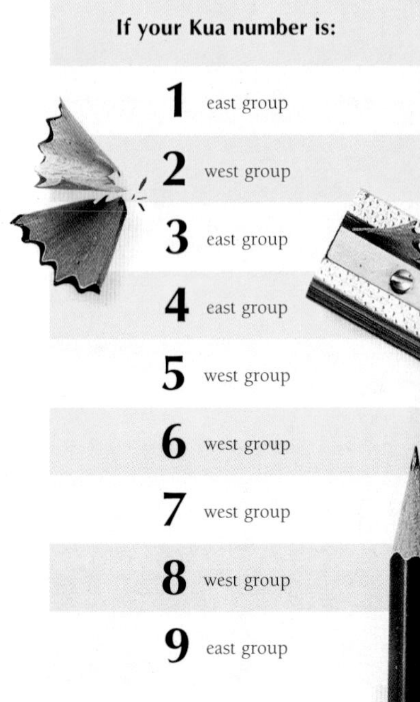

If your Kua number is:	
1	east group
2	west group
3	east group
4	east group
5	west group
6	west group
7	west group
8	west group
9	east group

a direction that allows the person to capture his or her Fu Wei. Doing this successfully leads to great success in any endeavor, which requires the enhancement of the intellect and the development of a skill or profession. It brings recognition, achievement, and success to those who genuinely work at securing this success. The Fu Wei direction imparts precious feng shui luck which considerably smoothes the way to success. Your child will feel energized and highly motivated and will catch the eye of teachers.

THE KUA FORMULA

To determine your orientation, first determine your Kua number

- Obtain your Chinese year of birth based on the calendar on pages 28–9 and use this calculation to get your Kua number.
- Add the last two digits of your Chinese year of birth. e.g. **1948, 4+8=12**.
- If the sum is higher than ten, reduce to a single digit, thus **1+2=3**.

Males: Subtract from **10**, thus **10-3=7**.
So, for men born in **1948**,
the Kua number is **7**.

Females: Add **5**, thus **3+5=8**.
So, for women born in **1948**,
the Kua number is **8**.

Now check against this table for your Fu Wei direction and location.

There is no 5 in this formula, though it is shown in the table for clarity. Females should use 2 instead of 5, and males 8.

Your Fu Wei orientation is:

NORTH for both males and females

SOUTHWEST for both males and females

EAST for both males and females

SOUTHEAST for both males and females

SOUTHWEST for males and
NORTHEAST for females

NORTHWEST for both males and females

WEST for both males and females

NORTHEAST for both males and females

SOUTH for both males and females

This formula is thus ideal for those who want to become grade A students and who have ambitions to climb to the very top of their profession. It is not for enhancing incomes as much as for personal growth and development, although implicit in this sort of luck is the promise of great success in the future.

THE CHINESE CALENDAR

Note that the Chinese New Year begins in either late January or early February. When calculating your Kua number, do take note of this. So if you were born in January 1946 before the New Year, your Chinese year of birth is 1945, not 1946. This calendar also indicates the ruling element of your year of birth. This gives you further clues to which corner of the home (based on your element) will have the most effect on your well-being.

Year	From	To	Element	Year	From	To	Element
1900	31 Jan 1900	18 Feb 1901	Metal	1923	16 Feb 1923	4 Feb 1924	Water
1901	19 Feb 1901	17 Feb 1902	Metal	1924	5 Feb 1924	24 Jan 1925	Wood
1902	18 Feb 1902	28 Jan 1903	Water	1925	25 Jan 1925	12 Feb 1926	Wood
1903	29 Jan 1903	15 Jan 1904	Water	1926	13 Feb 1926	1 Feb 1927	Fire
1904	16 Feb 1904	3 Feb 1905	Wood	1927	2 Feb 1927	22 Jan 1928	Fire
1905	4 Feb 1905	24 Jan1906	Wood	1928	23 Jan 1928	9 Feb 1929	Earth
1906	25 Jan 1906	12 Feb 1907	Fire	1929	10 Feb 1929	29 Jan 1930	Earth
1907	13 Feb 1907	1 Feb 1908	Fire	1930	30 Jan 1930	16 Feb 1931	Metal
1908	2 Feb 1908	21 Jan 1909	Earth	1931	17 Feb 1931	15 Feb 1932	Metal
1909	22 Jan 1909	9 Feb 1910	Earth	1932	16 Feb 1932	25 Jan 1933	Water
1910	10 Feb 1910	29 Jan 1911	Metal	1933	26 Jan 1933	13 Feb 1934	Water
1911	30 Jan 1911	17 Feb 1912	Metal	1934	14 Feb 1934	3 Feb 1935	Wood
1912	18 Feb 1912	25 Feb 1913	Water	1935	4 Feb 1935	23 Jan 1936	Wood
1913	26 Feb 1913	25 Jan 1914	Water	1936	24 Jan 1936	10 Feb 1937	Fire
1914	26 Jan 1914	13 Feb 1915	Wood	1937	11 Feb 1937	30 Jan 1938	Fire
1915	14 Feb 1915	2 Feb 1916	Wood	1938	31 Jan 1938	18 Feb 1939	Earth
1916	3 Feb 1916	22 Jan 1917	Fire	1939	19 Feb 1939	7 Feb 1940	Earth
1917	23 Jan 1917	10 Feb 1918	Fire	1940	8 Feb 1940	26 Jan 1941	Metal
1918	11 Feb 1918	31 Jan 1919	Earth	1941	27 Jan 1941	14 Feb 1942	Metal
1919	1 Feb 1919	19 Feb 1920	Earth	1942	15 Feb 1942	24 Feb 1943	Water
1920	20 Feb 1920	7 Feb 1921	Metal	1943	25 Feb 1943	24 Jan 1944	Water
1921	8 Feb 1921	27 Jan 1922	Metal	1944	25 Jan 1944	12 Feb 1945	Wood
1922	28 Jan 1922	15 Feb 1923	Water	1945	13 Feb 1945	1 Feb 1946	Wood

Year	From	To	Element	Year	From	To	Element
1946	2 Feb 1946	21 Jan 1947	Fire	1977	18 Feb 1977	6 Feb 1978	Fire
1947	22 Jan 1947	9 Feb 1948	Fire	1978	7 Feb 1978	27 Jan 1979	Earth
1948	10 Feb 1948	28 Jan 1949	Earth	1979	28 Jan 1979	15 Feb 1980	Earth
1949	29 Jan 1949	16 Feb 1950	Earth	1980	16 Feb 1980	4 Feb 1981	Metal
1950	17 Feb 1950	5 Feb 1951	Metal	1981	5 Feb 1981	24 Jan 1982	Metal
1951	6 Feb 1951	26 Jan 1952	Metal	1982	25 Jan 1982	12 Feb 1983	Water
1952	27 Jan 1952	13 Feb 1953	Water	1983	13 Feb 1983	1 Feb 1984	Water
1953	14 Feb 1953	2 Feb 1954	Water	1984	2 Feb 1984	19 Feb 1985	Wood
1954	3 Feb 1954	23 Jan 1955	Wood	1985	20 Feb 1985	8 Feb 1986	Wood
1955	24 Jan 1955	11 Feb 1956	Wood	1986	9 Feb 1986	28 Jan 1987	Fire
1956	12 Feb 1956	30 Jan 1957	Fire	1987	29 Jan 1987	16 Feb 1988	Fire
1957	31 Jan 1957	17 Feb 1958	Fire	1988	17 Feb 1988	5 Feb 1989	Earth
1958	18 Feb 1958	7 Feb 1959	Earth	1989	6 Feb 1989	26 Jan 1990	Earth
1959	8 Feb 1959	27 Jan 1960	Earth	1990	27 Jan 1990	14 Feb 1991	Metal
1960	28 Jan 1960	14 Feb 1961	Metal	1991	15 Feb 1991	3 Feb 1992	Metal
1961	15 Feb 1961	4 Feb 1962	Metal	1992	4 Feb 1992	22 Jan 1993	Water
1962	5 Feb 1962	24 Jan 1963	Water	1993	23 Jan 1993	9 Feb 1994	Water
1963	25 Jan 1963	12 Feb 1964	Water	1994	10 Feb 1994	30 Jan 1995	Wood
1964	13 Feb 1964	1 Feb 1965	Wood	1995	31 Jan 1995	18 Feb 1996	Wood
1965	2 Feb 1965	20 Jan 1966	Wood	1996	19 Feb 1996	7 Feb 1997	Fire
1966	21 Jan 1966	8 Feb 1967	Fire	1997	8 Feb 1997	27 Jan 1998	Fire
1967	9 Feb 1967	29 Jan 1968	Fire	1998	28 Jan 1998	15 Feb 1999	Earth
1968	30 Jan 1968	16 Feb 1969	Earth	1999	16 Feb 1999	4 Feb 2000	Earth
1969	17 Feb 1969	5 Feb 1970	Earth	2000	5 Feb 2000	23 Jan 2001	Metal
1970	6 Feb 1970	26 Jan 1971	Metal	2001	24 Jan 2001	11 Feb 2002	Metal
1971	27 Jan 1971	15 Feb 1972	Metal	2002	12 Feb 2002	31 Jan 2003	Water
1972	16 Feb 1972	22 Feb 1973	Water	2003	1 Feb 2003	21 Jan 2004	Water
1973	23 Feb 1973	22 Jan 1974	Water	2004	22 Jan 2004	8 Feb 2005	Wood
1974	23 Jan 1974	10 Feb 1975	Wood	2005	9 Feb 2005	28 Jan 2006	Wood
1975	11 Feb 1975	30 Jan 1976	Wood	2006	29 Jan 2006	17 Feb 2007	Fire
1976	31 Jan 1976	17 Feb 1977	Fire	2007	18 Feb 2007	6 Feb 2008	Fire

When using formula feng shui it is essential to be very accurate in your measurements and also when taking compass directions. Note the elements that are represented in each of the directions.

APPLYING THE KUA FORMULA

The home should be demarcated into the nine sectors according to the Lo Shu grid as shown. To do this accurately, use a good measuring tape and try to get the demarcations as accurate as possible.

Next, get your bearings and identify the eight corners according to their compass directions. Please note that although feng shui books usually place south at the top according to Chinese tradition, the actual directions referred to are identical with those used in the West. Thus the Chinese north is exactly the same as the north indicated by any Western-style compass. So you can use a good Western compass and, standing in the center of your home, identify the eight side locations by dividing the floor space of the home into a grid of nine equal squares. Draw out the floor plan of your home, as this will assist in the arrangement of rooms and furniture.

Even as you identify the sectors, keep the matching elements of each compass location at the back of your mind. This is because the application of the five element theory transcends every school of feng shui, and irrespective of the method or formula being used, it is necessary to remember this. For ease of reference, the elements are indicated in each of the sectors. This is according to the Later Heaven Arrangement of the trigrams, the arrangement always used for the living. The element of the center is earth.

Please note that rooms do not necessarily all fit neatly into the Lo Shu grid. Most rooms fall within two or even three sectors. This is when the exact placement of important pieces of furniture, such as desks and beds, in the room becomes extremely important.

ACTIVATING THE FU WEI DIRECTION

Once you know your child's personal Fu Wei direction and you have demarcated your floor area according to the Lo Shu square, there are several ways you can start to match his or her human chi energies with that of the surrounding space. The Fu Wei direction can be activated to attract auspicious sheng chi for personal benefit.

Check the Fu Wei direction based on his or her Kua number from the table on page 25. This is also the luckiest compass location for your child's bedroom. Tapping the Fu Wei allows your child to sleep, eat, and study well, without succumbing to the stresses and strains of work or exams. Incorporating this formula into his or her personal feng shui is also a very effective safeguard against carelessness, ill health, and laziness.

N

Child's bedroom

The ideal way of capturing good study luck with this method is to try to match all the most important doors in the home according to your child's Fu Wei, but this is hardly practical. Nor is it very clever; other members of the family must also be taken care of and account must be taken of the overall luck of the family. Leave the main door into the home for other feng shui features that benefit every member of the family, especially the breadwinner or head of the household.

Concentrate, instead, on using your child's personal Fu Wei direction for his or her room. The direction your child faces when sleeping, sitting, and working should follow his or her personal auspicious direction. This means working with the following:

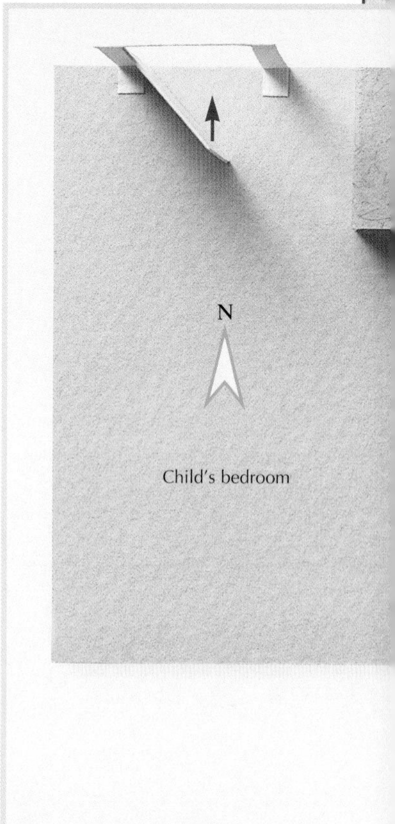

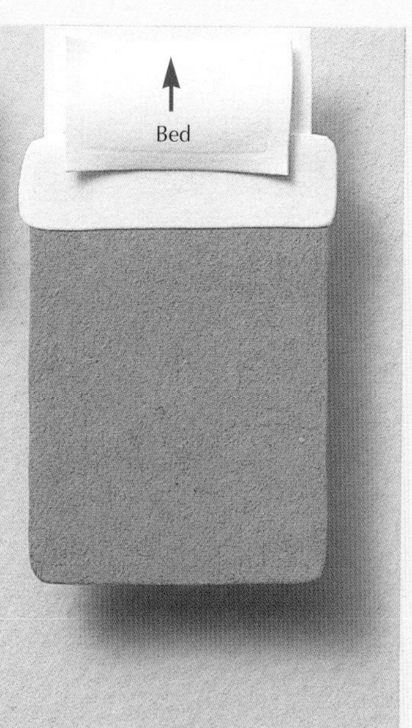

The arrows indicate how the sleeping and working directions should be oriented. Note that for sleeping, where the head points is vital, and for sitting down to work, where the head faces is important. In this example, even the door into the bedroom points to the Fu Wei direction; this is excellent, but it is not always possible to get everything right. Two out of three is fine!

THE FU WEI DIRECTION IN PRACTICE

For example, if your child's Fu Wei direction is north, this is how he or she should sleep and work.

- The door into his or her bedroom.
- The placement of his or her bed to tap the best sleeping direction.
- The placement of the desk to tap the best working direction.

IN THE GARDEN

Extend element theory into the garden. Install a high light in the northeast corner of the garden to activate education luck for your children. Repeat this garden light also in the south, which represents the luck of recognition. This attracts success luck in examinations and should be of assistance when your children apply for

such things as scholarships and study grants. Do this early in your child's school career and let the effect be felt gradually over the following years.

ACTIVATING FU WEI IN SCHOOL AND IN COLLEGE

The auspicious direction can be applied all through life. Carry a small compass everywhere you go and develop the habit of always taking directions. This makes it easy to identify your best education direction each time you sit down to take an exam. If possible, choose a desk in the classroom that is auspicious for you.

At university, simply move the position of the desk and bed in your room to tap into this powerful method of feng shui. Even if you do nothing else except guard against feng shui's killing breath, your hard work will be handsomely rewarded with excellent academic success.

A simple pocket compass, like those used by Boy Scouts, is an enormously valuable aid for enhancing your education luck.

PRACTICAL PROBLEMS

Rooms are rarely regular square or rectangular shapes, making it difficult in practice to superimpose a nine-sector grid. The problem of missing corners is still more serious. If the education corner is missing as a result of an en suite bathroom or simply by the shape of the room, your study luck could be seriously undermined. In this case, it might be better to change rooms or implement a feng shui cure, depending on the circumstances. Three of the easiest ways of correcting an irregular-shaped room are shown here. However, correcting the problem merely improves the situation; it is much more difficult to create the good study luck you want.

Installing a light to illuminate the missing sector will help.

THE WORKING DIRECTION

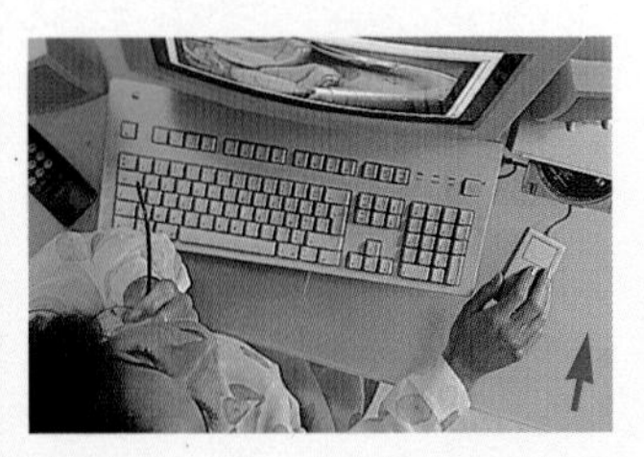

This is one of the most vital determinants of any type of auspicious luck (watch the arrow). Try to work sitting and facing your personal education and self-development direction. It is a good idea to draw an arrow on your desk to remind you always to face that way when doing an assignment or working on a project.

The examples shown are floor areas with an irregular layout. If you superimpose the nine sector grid onto the room and take directions from the center, you will immediately see which compass sector is missing from the room and set about rectifying the problem.

According to feng shui, missing corners mean that the room will be lacking in certain luck aspects. This analysis can also be applied to the entire home. The types of luck missing depend on the corresponding compass directions of missing sectors. If one missing sector represents your education direction, you can partially correct the matter by one of the following actions.

- Install a light.
- Hang a mirror on the wall.
- Build an extension.

What you do depends on your circumstances and whether you have the available space.

Building an extension is the best cure, but this depends on the space available.

A mirror on the wall extends it outward, thereby correcting the problem.

An irregular layout sometimes makes it difficult to have the working desk located in your best corner. If you cannot get the location, tapping the direction is often good enough. This means you should work facing your best study direction. If you cannot tap either the location or direction, do try to work facing one of your three other auspicious directions.

EAST AND WEST GROUP DIRECTIONS

Compass feng shui divides the human race into east and west group people. Every person is said to have four favorable directions, with each direction representing a different kind of auspicious luck. In addition to the personal development direction, you will have three other auspicious directions. All these favorable directions belong to the same east or west group, so it is easy to establish what your three good directions are. The east group directions are east, north, south, and southeast.
The west group directions are west, southwest, northwest, and northeast. East group directions are bad for west group people and west group directions are harmful for east group people. This principle is also true for locations.

The group you belong to depends on your Kua number. East group people have Kua numbers one, three, four, and nine. West group people have Kua numbers two, five, six, seven, and eight.

SE	S	SW
E		W
NE	N	NW

It is important to remember your unlucky directions, especially when arranging your sitting, working, and sleeping directions. Try drawing out your personalized Kua chart as shown. For example, if your Kua number is eight, your Kua chart will look like this, with the inauspicious directions marked in blue and the auspicious directions marked in red.

KUA NUMBER	east/west group
1	east group
2	west group
3	east group
4	east group
5	west group for males
5	west group for females
6	west group
7	west group
8	west group
9	east group

YOUR UNFAVORABLE DIRECTIONS

The compass formula also informs you of the directions that will hurt you. These four bad directions are different for each of the Kua numbers and they vary in the intensity of bad luck they bring.

- The Ho Hai direction brings bad luck. Your efforts bring no results.
- The Wu Kwei direction brings five ghosts to your doorstep. People in authority intimidate you.
- The Lui Shar direction attacks you with six killings. Every move you make is plagued with bad luck.
- The Chueh Mung direction is the most severe of all. It means total loss.

This table shows you the four harmful directions according to your Kua number.

Ho Hai direction	**Wu Kwei** direction	**Lui Shar** direction	**Chueh Ming** direction
West	Northeast	Northwest	Southwest
East	Southeast	South	North
Southwest	Northwest	Northeast	West
Northwest	Southwest	West	Northeast
East	Southeast	South	North
South	North	East	Southeast
Southeast	East	North	South
North	South	Southeast	East
South	North	East	Southeast
Northeast	West	Southwest	Northwest

FENG SHUI SAFEGUARDS

保護

Feng shui offers guidelines on the placement of bedrooms and arrangement of furniture that can provide safeguards to protect your children from being inadvertently struck by the shar chi, that causes them to succumb to pressure and sickness. If your child is frequently sick, investigate the living space in his or her bedroom. Check the placement of the bed and observe the following simple rules.

BEDROOM LAYOUT

In addition to the suggestions illustrated, the bed should never be placed directly beneath an overhead beam. This is severely harmful. It should not be placed directly in front of the door, in either direction. Always stay clear of the door, especially if the door itself faces another door, a staircase, mirror, or toilet.

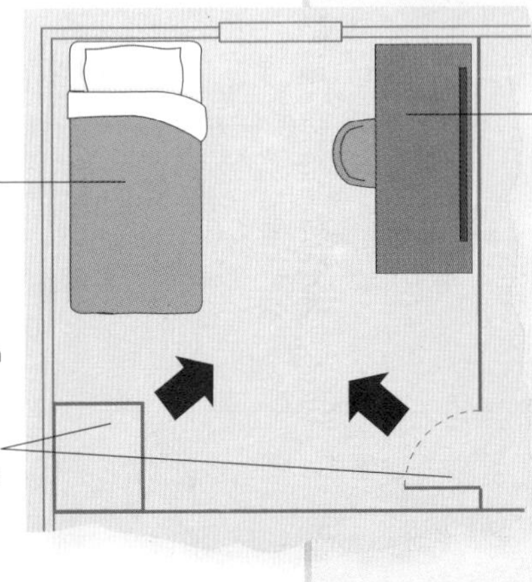

The bed placed diagonally across from the door is excellent. The position is also good in relation to the windows.

Harmful shar chi emanating from the corner pillar in this room is not hurting the bed. Never place the bed directly in the path of the sharp edge of such pillars.

A dressing table with a mirror positioned to face the bed is not advisable. Remove the mirror. The rule is never to sleep with a mirror facing the bed In children's bedrooms, this can cause sickness.

Try to avoid putting your children in triangular, odd-shaped, or L-shaped bedrooms.

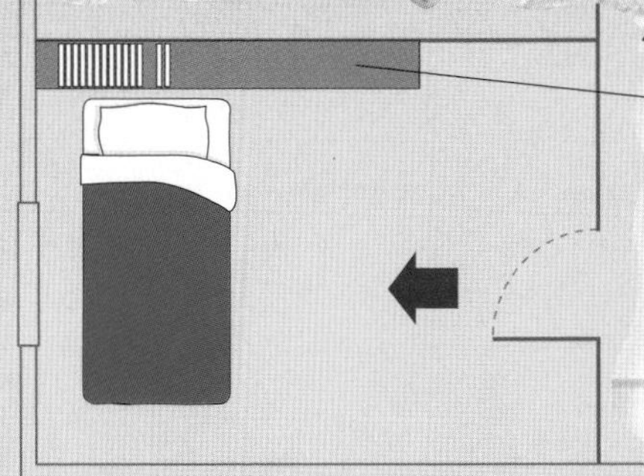

open bookshelves

Open bookshelves above a headboard cause the occupant headaches and insomnia. Concentration is seriously affected. The bed placed directly in line with the door is harmful and it is worse if there is a window directly facing the door. All the luck flies out the window.

When there are several children in a household, try to avoid having their bedrooms along a long corridor. Too many doors opening off a corridor causes quarrels between siblings. When doors face each other in a confrontational way, it also causes quarrels and misunderstandings.

The bed should not 'float' in the middle of a room. A desk next to the headboard is not advisable. The door behind is an unlucky feature.

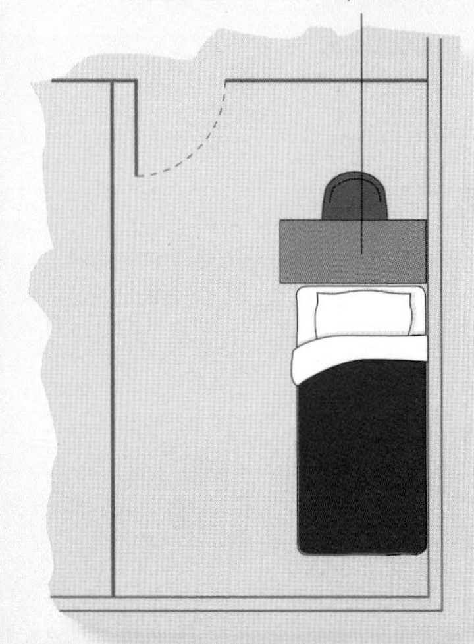

Sleeping with the headboard against a wall with a toilet on the other side is especially harmful to the physical well-being of the occupant. It is advisable to avoid this kind of placement for the bed. According to feng shui, even if the head is pointing toward the sleeper's best direction, harmful shar chi created in the toilet will cause bad luck and problems. Sleeping directly underneath a toilet in an upper room is equally harmful.

ASPIRING TO BE A SUCCESSFUL STUDENT

Perhaps the most exciting promise of feng shui is its potential to turn average, but hard-working, students into high-fliers. Feng shui works at various levels. If the living space has been properly activated with good feng shui, children become self-motivated and are keen to perform to the best of their ability. Study skills and attitudes improve substantially and conscientious hard work pays off with excellent examination results. Grades start to improve dramatically.

THE SITTING DIRECTION

Sit with the head facing the best study direction and with solid support behind. A painting of a mountain is excellent. Do not sit directly in front of the window. This symbolizes a lack of support.

In addition to observing the compass directions and activating the education corners of the home and bedroom, it is also necessary to comply with a few feng shui rules in order to be protected against bad feng shui. It is especially important to ensure that when the child sits down to work or study, he or she is always protected against poison arrows and that there is solid support behind. This can be in the form of a wall, closet, or picture of a rounded mountain. Avoid hanging paintings of water (lakes or waterfalls, for example) or placing any hostile or pointed object behind. Pictures of guns, cannons, planes, cars, and wild animals should be strenuously avoided.

While working, make certain nothing sharp or pointed, such as the edge of a closet or a protruding corner is hitting at the chair. This creates shar chi, which harms the child. Also make sure that there are no beams or edges above.

FENG SHUI DURING EXAMINATIONS AND INTERVIEWS

The auspicious direction method can, and indeed should, be activated in other situations. Whenever possible, let your child face this direction

- When doing his or her homework or when revising.
- When sitting for an examination.
- When attending lectures or in class.
- When attending interviews.

LOOKING OUT THE WINDOW

If the study desk is positioned so that the child looks out of the window and is directly facing an oncoming road, a dead tree, or the edge of a large building, the view can be the source of severe shar chi. Use heavy drapes to block it out.

THINGS TO BE ALERT TO

It is important to remember that the luck of the good direction by itself does not represent any protection against shar chi caused by beams, pillars, and sharp edges. These are structural features present in any building and it is important to develop a habit of always noticing where they are, so that you can avoid them.

In addition, you should also be alert to the less obvious structures, features, and objects that may be sending out secret poison arrows. For instance, if there are paintings of guns hanging on the walls, these send out negative energy. Paintings,

EXAMS

Examination success depends above all on thorough and conscientious preparation. But sitting in an auspicious direction, protected from the harmful effects of any poison arrows that may be in the room, will ensure the best results possible.

Trees too close to the window, thereby blocking off the sunlight, create excessive yin energy which can be harmful. They need to be chopped down or at least cut back. However, if trees are not too close and look healthy and the direction outside is the east, they can be a most auspicious view. Just make certain trees never block out the sun completely. If the trees are in your garden, trim them each year to maintain good balance and harmony.

especially abstracts, that seem negative or hostile can be disastrous. For example, Picasso's Weeping Woman is a particularly bad painting to hang anywhere near children. The defensive dimension of feng shui should never be ignored. Even if everything else is correct, the killing breath of symbolic poison arrows is extremely harmful and it can, in certain circumstances, be lethal.

Carry a compass everywhere and when attending lectures, try to sit facing your study direction, that is, your Fu Wei direction. If this is not possible, at least make certain that you do not sit facing one of your four unlucky directions, as this will simply drain you of energy, thereby affecting your powers of concentration. Let the energies around work for you, rather than against you.

During exam times, be extra careful with your sitting direction. Check the orientation of the room and, if possible, swivel your chair so that you take your examination facing at least one of your four auspicious directions. This will ensure that your sitting direction is in harmony with the energies that surround you during that crucial testing time.

Wall paintings of guns, or other hostile objects, can have a very negative effect in a classroom, study, or examination room.

MAINTAINING YIN AND YANG BALANCE

Another dimension of feng shui is the need to maintain yin and yang balance. These are the two primordial forces that are opposite and yet complementary. Good feng shui can only exist when yin and yang are in harmony with each other.

To understand yin-yang balance, it is important to know that Chinese belief maintains that one gives existence to the other. Thus yin is darkness, night, cold, quiet, and stillness. Yang, on the other hand, is daylight, brightness, warmth, heat, sounds, and activity. Without the cold of yin, there is no yang warmth, and without yang sunshine there can be no yin moonlight. Another attribute of the yin-yang cosmology is that one force contains the seed of the other complementary force. In yang there must always be a little bit of yin, and vice versa.

In feng shui, the yin-yang balance requires the simultaneous presence of both forces. When there is an excess of either, the space affected is said to be unbalanced. In such a situation, there just cannot be any good luck. However, because we are dealing with life energy when we speak of yang feng shui, it is vital that the environment must always have yang energy and should never be too yin. When the environment is too yin, lethargy, apathy, a sense of defeat, and even death could well be the outcome. At the same time, do not eliminate yin altogether. Maintaining this delicate balance between the two forces is at the root of feng shui.

This symbol of yin and yang symbolizes the universe being in a constant state of flux and change. Yin becomes yang and yang becomes yin in a never-ending cycle.

There are two basic aspects to the requirements of balance when considering education luck. The first addresses the universal direction that represents education; this is northeast. The second concerns the Fu Wei direction of individual students. Although a balance of yin and yang is vital, it is necessary that the two directions that have a direct impact on education luck should never suffer from excessive yin or excessive yang energy.

This happens when trees are allowed to grow out of hand, thereby completely blocking out the sunlight. If the foliage creates too much shade and darkness, the situation has definitely become too yin, to an extent that it has become harmful. Inside the home, space becomes too yin where rooms are damp and cold. This usually happens when store rooms or unoccupied rooms are not properly maintained. Never allow rooms to remain dark, cold, and damp for long periods. This is never good feng shui for the home and the children of the household are usually the first to be affected.

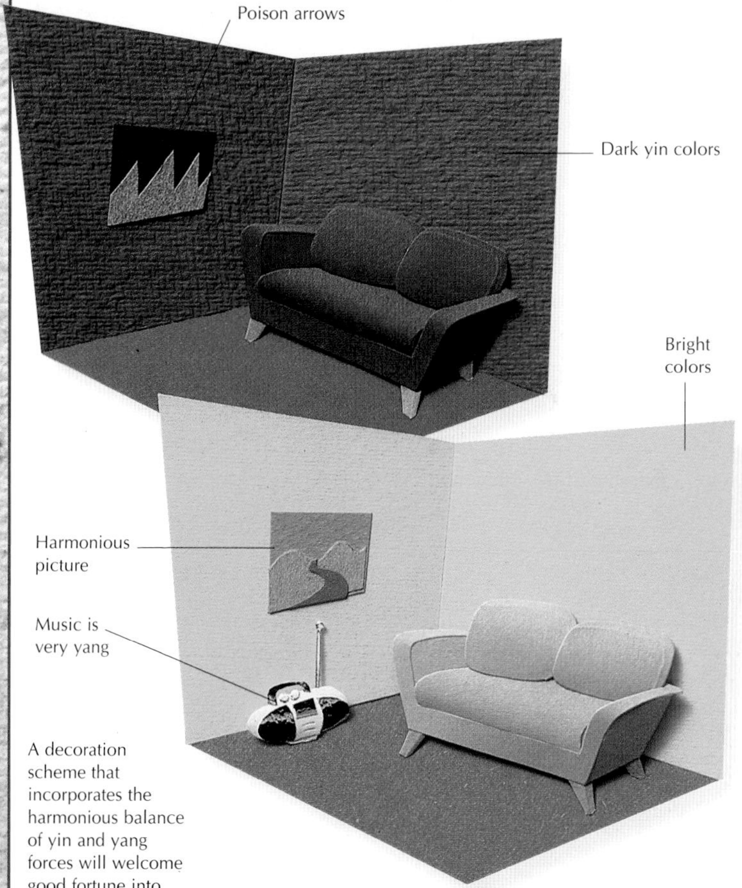

Poison arrows

Dark yin colors

Bright colors

Harmonious picture

Music is very yang

A decoration scheme that incorporates the harmonious balance of yin and yang forces will welcome good fortune into your home.

All the rooms in the home should always have a healthy dose of yang energy. This is conducive to proper growth and development. Paint rooms in white or bright colors. Keep the radio turned on through the day. Install a music system or hang little chimes that make tinkling sounds. Finally, air the rooms of your home regularly, as this clears the air and keeps the energies fresh.

HAZARDS AND HOW TO SPOT THEM

THE CHANGING ENVIRONMENT

危險

Much of feng shui practice is getting accustomed to spotting structural features inside and outside the home which can harm members of the family. It is often easy to overlook this defensive aspect. Hazards in the immediate external environment require the main entrance door into the home to be protected. Inside the home, hazards are created by structural pillars, beams, the layout of the rooms, and the arrangement of furniture. It is, therefore, necessary to familiarize yourself with at least some of the more common dangers that may inadvertently threaten to destroy all the good feng shui so painstakingly put in. In fact, it is advisable to be aware of changes in the environment in and around the home so that the family's feng shui is never at serious risk.

Feng shui is not a static exercise. Because the energies within the environment are constantly changing, living in a state of awareness is important. For example, when trees are small they blend in beautifully with the surroundings, but as they grow, the energies emitted are expanded, eventually causing imbalance not only of yin and yang, but also in the five element cosmology. In the same way, new roads, new buildings, and infrastructure developments will always have a strong feng shui significance.

There are two aspects to being alert to the changing forces in the environment. The first concerns being aware of physical changes and the second has to do with intangible forces caused by nothing more than the passage of time. Both aspects are dealt with in this book.

New roads can create potentially hazardous poison arrows. It is important to be attuned to these types of changes in our surroundings because they may affect home and family.

THE BRIGHT HALL

Feng shui often speaks of the benefits that accrue from having an empty space in front of the home. Such an empty space – a park, football field, or playground – allows the beneficial and benign sheng chi to accumulate and settle before entering your home, bringing good fortune with it. The phrase used to describe this feature is the bright hall. When there is a bright hall in front of your main door, your family will enjoy great good fortune and all plans will proceed smoothly.

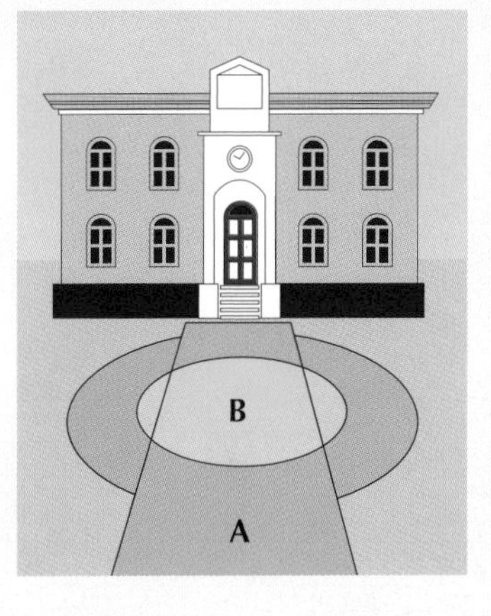

Schools and colleges with a playing field or empty land located directly in front of the main entrance usually produce excellent graduates. This good fortune is caused by the bright hall effect, which brings excellent feng shui to the school. However, if there is a straight road leading directly toward the main gate **A**, the effect is extremely inauspicious. It is far better to have a circular driveway, as this slows down the energy coming toward the building **B**. Good chi always moves slowly. Bad chi always moves fast.

PHYSICAL CHANGES IN THE LANDSCAPE

A new highway overpass will definitely hurt your family if it seems to cut into your home. For rooms that face such an overpass, the harmful hostile energies will be too strong, causing severe bad luck. The construction of a new high-rise building also affects the feng shui of a home. If the new building blocks the main door, the effect will be negative. If it rises behind your home, thereby symbolizing solid support, then the effect is good feng shui. Generally, as most infrastructure projects are massive, they cause severe bad luck when they are located in front of your home.

LOCATION OF TOILETS, STORAGE SPACE, AND GARAGES

A very common cause of specific types of bad luck can often be traced to the location of these rooms within the home. It is necessary to be particularly careful about the toilet because it literally flushes away all the good luck represented by the corner in which it is located. Thus if it is located in the education and study luck corner of the home – the northeast – students living there will suffer from bad luck in their studies and examinations.

A toilet located in the personal Fu Wei direction of particular family members is equally harmful. If there is a bathroom and toilet en suite in your child's room, do make sure it is not located in his or her Fu Wei direction or the northeast. If it is, reduce usage of this particular toilet and keep it closed. Better still, re-locate the toilet altogether.

The best way to deal with the problem is always to keep toilet doors closed. Make toilets within the home small and unobtrusive, so they make up only a small part of any corner. If you have a large bath and dressing area, screen off the toilet itself so that it is not easily visible.

Toilets should be carefully located, and it is best to keep the door shut when the toilet is not in use.

Books are central to all educational achievement and should be treated with respect.

Store rooms are not as harmful as toilets, but when mops, brooms, and other cleaning paraphernalia are placed in store rooms in full view of the front door, they serve to chase away the good fortune chi that enters the home. Keep your store rooms closed and all brooms stowed away.

Never prop up a broom or mop in the education or relevant Fu Wei corners of the home, since these symbolically sweep away all the good luck of the corner. Try not to have the store room in this corner, and never sleep above, or directly below, a store room.

For study luck, never leave text books on the floor or in the toilet. Treat them with respect. Place them on a table, desk, or on shelves. They should always be higher than the ground. Never allow anyone to step over your text books.

Clutter of any sort is always frowned upon by feng shui masters.

When a bedroom is directly above a garage, the person is sleeping above a 'room' with no substance and is therefore unlikely to experience good luck.

Keep brooms and mops hidden or they will sweep your good luck away.

There cannot be good balance when there are dirty clothes, stale food (very yin), and dirt around. They are not conducive to attracting the good sheng chi.

At all costs, avoid locating a bedroom or any important room directly above the garage. This suggests that you are sleeping on no substance! If your child's bedroom is situated above the family garage, it is difficult for him or her to enjoy much good luck at all, as a result of which performance will always be below expectations and capabilities. Indeed, as a general rule, no one should sleep above a garage or an empty space. Hillside, split level homes that are built on exposed piles are said to have unlucky feng shui unless the piles are plastered up into the rooms.

TOILETS

In the old days in China, palaces and wealthy homes had no toilets. Servants brought in tubs for bathing and toilets were carried in and out whenever needed. The poorer peasants who lived in the country also did not have toilets inside the home.

THE FENG SHUI OF KITCHENS

The placement of a kitchen can also undermine a family's fortunes. It is thus important to make sure that no cooking or washing of dishes is done in the corner of the home that represents the type of luck you want, particularly not in the education corner if you have children who are still of school or college age.

THE COOKER

The good name of the family and its members gets seriously hurt when the cooker is inauspiciously located. Feng shui always advises that a cooker should never be located in the northwest or north. It should also not be in a place that corresponds with your family's personal auspicious directions. It is always better to place it in your unlucky location.

The cooker's source of energy (electricity or gas) should come from the direction that represents your auspicious direction. If the oven door faces your child's Fu Wei direction, he or she will gain high academic honors. If it is not possible to tap the Fu Wei direction, try to arrange it to face one of the other three auspicious directions. At all costs, avoid having the cooker facing any one of your child's four inauspicious directions, as this could lead to scandals, expulsions, and a fall from grace. To protect your family from mishaps, try to observe as many of these guidelines as possible.

SIMPLE GUIDELINES ON

It should never be placed awkwardly or in a corner.

It should not be sandwiched between two sinks or water faucets. This symbolizes tears within the family caused by a severe misfortune or loss.

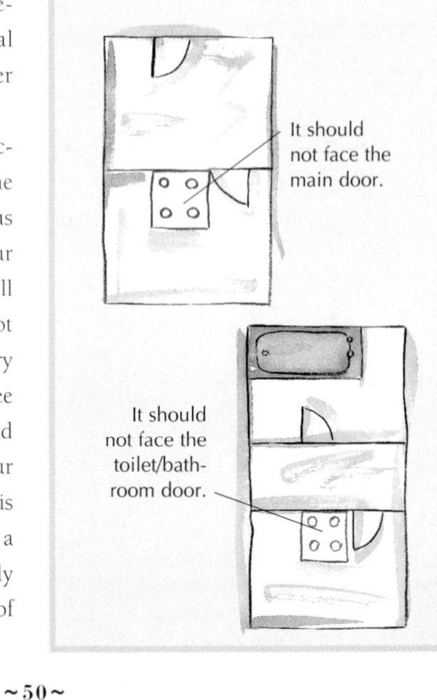

LOCATING THE COOKER

TIPS ON KITCHEN LOCATION

- The kitchen should never be located in the center of the home. This generally damages the family's luck, especially that of the head of the household – the breadwinner.
- A toilet should not directly face the kitchen; nor should there be a toilet above it.
- The level of the kitchen should not be higher or lower than the dining area. It should definitely not be lower than the living area.
- The shape of the kitchen must not be round and nor should it be irregular. A rectangular shape is the best.
- A kitchen is best placed in the inner half of a home. If it is placed too near the main door, family luck will be dissolved.
- A kitchen is luckier placed on the right of the main door. If it is placed on the left or directly in line with the main door, there tends to be many quarrels between husband and wife.

THE TIME DIMENSION

USING FLYING STAR FENG SHUI

時间

This particular school of feng shui addresses the changes wrought in feng shui over time. This popular method is widely used in Hong Kong, Malaysia, and Singapore. The time aspects of feng shui complement the space dimension of other feng shui methods. Flying star thus adds the vital dynamics of the time factor. This is a very advanced method and it is not really necessary for amateur practitioners to get too involved in the technical details of its computations. However, it is useful to have a reference table to enable you to investigate the impact of flying star on your own feng shui, particularly since this method is excellent for warning against the flying stars that bring serious bad luck. Being forewarned is often a great way of avoiding bad luck.

WHAT ARE THE FLYING STARS?

The stars refer to the numbers one to nine placed around a nine-sector grid, known as the Lo Shu magic square. The numbers around the grid fly – they change over time. The way they do this forms the crux of this method of feng shui.

Every day, month, and year and every 20-year period has its own arrangement of numbers around the square. Every number has its own meanings and tells the feng shui expert who knows how to interpret the numbers, a great many things. For the purpose of getting warnings, it is sufficient to monitor the period and year stars.

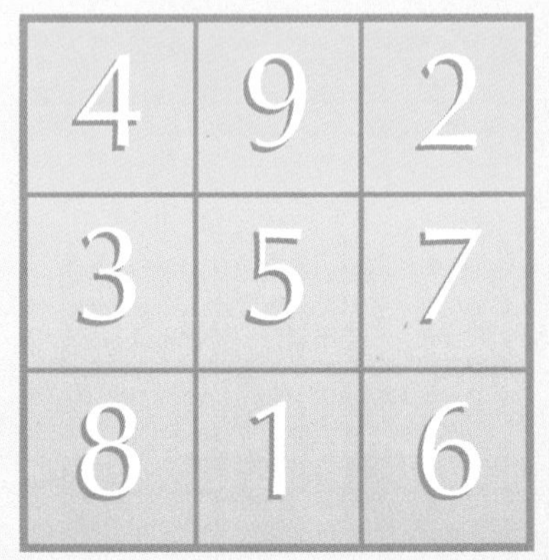

THE PERIOD OF SEVEN

We are currently living through the period of seven, which started in 1984 and does not end until the year 2003. This means that during this period, the number seven is deemed to be very lucky. The Lo Shu square for this period is shown here. Through an interpretation of the numbers, it describes the fortunate and less fortunate sectors up to the year 2003.

SOUTH

6	2	4
5	7	9
1	3	8

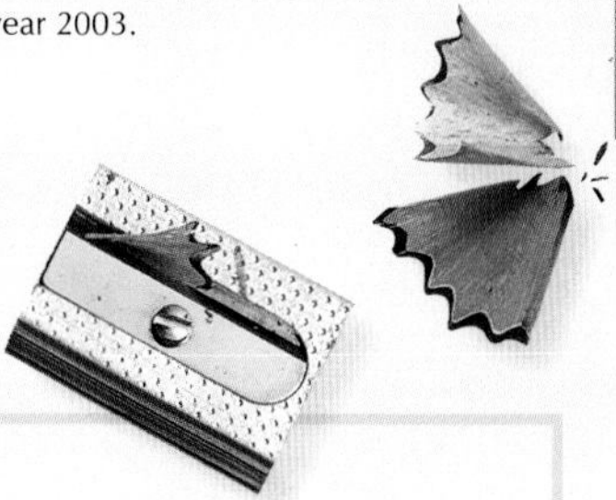

During the period of seven, the bad-luck star number five is located in the east. This is interpreted to mean that if the main door of your home is located in the east, you should be very careful during this 20-year period. It also means that those sleeping in bedrooms located in the east should also be extra careful against being stabbed in the back.

The analysis will be more accurate when investigation is also conducted on the star numerals during the month and the year in question. When two or all three star numerals are fives in the same sector, loss due to extreme bad luck is certain during that month and year for anyone whose bedroom is in the sector where the fives occur together! When you become aware of the time when you need to be extra careful, one way of countering the bad luck is to travel away from home. Go for a vacation during that period, thereby avoiding the bad luck.

The original nine-sector Lo Shu square has the number five in the center. The numbers have been arranged so that the sum of any three numbers, taken vertically, horizontally, or diagonally, is 15. In flying star feng shui, the numbers move from grid to grid and they are then interpreted according to which of them is in which square. Each of the eight sectors on the outside of the square represents a corner of the home. For analysis, the center is the ninth sector. South is placed at the top according to tradition, for presentation purposes only. Use a simple compass to identify the actual corners of your home.

Year	Star numeral 2 is in the	Star numeral 5 is in the
1997	Southeast	West
1998	Center	Northeast
1999	Northwest	South
2000	West	North
2001	East	Southwest
2002	South	East
2003	North	Southeast
2004	Southwest	Center
2005	East	Northwest
2006	Southeast	West

Year	Month 1	Month 2	Month 3	Month 4	Month 5
1997	Southwest	East Northwest	Southeast West	Northeast	South Northwest
1998	Northeast	Northwest South	West North	Northeast Southwest	South East
1999	Northeast Southwest	South East	North Southeast	Southwest	East Northwest
2000	Southwest	East Northwest	Southeast West	Northeast	Northwest South
2001	Northeast	Northwest South	West North	Northeast Southwest	South East

ROOMS TO AVOID DURING SPECIFIC PERIODS

The yearly reference table
(**based on the lunar year*)

The table opposite shows where the star five and star two occur together. The star two combined with five makes it extra dangerous. The two stars may also bring sickness.

THE MONTHLY REFERENCE TABLES.

(*based on the lunar months)

The table below indicates the dangerous sectors during each of the 12 lunar months over the next five years. These are the sectors where the star numerals two and five are located during that month. In the years 1998 and 2001 there are 13 months, so one of the months has been doubled.

Match where the star numerals two and five fall during the months indicated with those of the annual star numerals and the 20-year period star numerals.

Where twos and fives occur together is when that sector becomes dangerous and anyone occupying a room in an afflicted sector would do well to leave it for that time. Be particularly careful when the star numerals two and five fall into the east sector. This is because this is the sector afflicted with the five in the 20-year period flying star. The danger months and the directions are marked. When there are two dots, it means that both the sectors indicated are dangerous.

Based on the reference table left, rooms in the south are prone to sickness in 1999. In 2002 rooms in the south and east should be avoided, and in 2005 rooms in the east.

Month 6	Month 7	Month 8	Month 9	Month 10	Month 11	Month 12
West North	Northeast Southwest	South East	North Southeast	Southwest	East Northwest	Southeast West
South East	North Southeast	Southwest	East Northwest	Southeast West	Northeast	Northwest South
Southeast West	Northeast	Northwest South	West North	Northeast Southwest	South East	North Southeast
West North	Northeast Southwest	South East	North Southeast	Southwest	East Northwest	Southeast West
North Southeast	Southwest	East Northwest	Southeast West	Northeast	Northwest South	West North

INDEX

FURTHER READING

Kwok, Man-Ho and O'Brien, Joanne, *The Elements of Feng Shui,* ELEMENT BOOKS, SHAFTESBURY, 1991

Lo, Raymond *Feng Shui: The Pillars of Destiny (Understanding Your Fate and Fortune),* TIMES EDITIONS, SINGAPORE, 1995

Skinner, Stephen, *Living Earth Manual of Feng Shui: Chinese Geomancy,* PENGUIN, 1989

Too, Lillian, *Basic Feng Shui,* KONSEP BOOKS, KUALA LUMPUR, 1997

Too, Lillian, *The Complete Illustrated Guide to Feng Shui,* ELEMENT BOOKS, SHAFTESBURY, 1996

Too, Lillian, *Chinese Astrology for Romance and Relationships,* KONSEP BOOKS, KUALA LUMPUR, 1996

Too, Lillian *Chinese Numerology in Feng Shui,* KONSEP BOOKS, KUALA LUMPUR, 1994

Too, Lillian, *Dragon Magic,* KONSEP BOOKS, KUALA LUMPUR, 1996

Too, Lillian *Feng Shui,* KONSEP BOOKS, KUALA LUMPUR, 1993

Too, Lillian *Practical Applications for Feng Shui,* KONSEP BOOKS, KUALA LUMPUR, 1994

Too, Lillian *Water Feng Shui for Wealth,* KONSEP BOOKS, KUALA LUMPUR, 1995

Walters, Derek *Feng Shui Handbook: A Practical Guide to Chinese Geomancy and Environmental Harmony,* AQUARIAN PRESS, 1991

USEFUL ADDRESSES

Feng Shui Design Studio
PO Box 705, Glebe, Sydney, NSW 2037, Australia, Tel: 61 2 315 8258

Feng Shui Society of Australia
PO Box 1565, Rozelle, Sydney NSW 2039, Australia

The Geomancer
The Feng Shui Store
PO Box 250, Woking, Surrey GU21 1YJ
Tel: 44 1483 839898
Fax: 44 1483 488998

Feng Shui Association
31 Woburn Place, Brighton BN1 9GA, Tel/Fax: 44 1273 693844

Feng Shui Network International
PO Box 2133, London W1A 1RL,
Tel: 44 171 935 8935,
Fax: 44 171 935 9295

The School of Feng Shui
34 Banbury Road, Ettington, Stratford-upon-Avon, Warwickshire CV37 7SU. Tel/Fax: 44 1789 740116

The Feng Shui Institute of America
PO Box 488, Wabasso, FL 32970,
Tel: 1 407 589 9900 Fax: 1 407 589 1611

Feng Shui Warehouse
PO Box 3005, San Diego, CA 92163,
Tel: 1 800 399 1599 Fax: 1 800 997 9831

"I want to say special words
of thanks to my Editor, **Caro Ness**
who has done an absolutely
brilliant job tightening my
manuscripts yet staying so true
to the essence of each of the
subjects of the nine books.
I must also acknowledge the vision
of **Julia McCutchen** whose belief
in this series was what brought out
the best in me. Thank you both."

Other titles in the Feng Shui Fundamentals series are:

Careers
Children
Eight Easy Lessons
Fame
Health
Love
Networking
Wealth